Days and Dreams

Emma Kelly

BookLeaf Publishing

Presentation by *BookLeaf Publishing*

Web: www.bookleafpub.com

E-mail: info@bookleafpub.com

ISBN: 9789357214827

First edition 2023

John, Cara, Rose and Oisin Kelly

When December Comes Around

I love when December comes around
And the leaves are wilting on the ground
While many people long for the summer
It's in the winter when I feel warmer

The winter brings the early nights
And the twinkling of Christmas lights
The magical hopes and expectations
Children looking forward to Christmas vacation

Christmas trees giving off their sparkling glow
While family gather round to share and grow
There really is no better time of year
With loved ones, past and present to hold dear.

So snuggle down deep in the bed tonight
Keeping all your hopes and dreams in sight
Christmas is surely on its way
When we will laugh, dance, sing and play.

If I Wasn't Me

If I wasn't me
I would know how to say No
If I wasn't me
People wouldn't hurt me so

If I wasn't me
I would look after number one
If I wasn't me
No harm would be done

If I wasn't me
The overthinking would cease
If I wasn't me
Maybe I would have peace

But I am me
And it is as such
I am me
The me that gives too much

Do I want to change?
I don't really know!
Do I want to change?
How would that go?

A little at a time
Take it day-by-day
What's meant to be
Will find a way

Home is Where the Heart Is

Home is where the heart is,
Isn't that what they say?
It's not the bricks and mortar,
Or the high pressure job every day.

The people that matter,
Who are always by your side.
The children you've nurtured,
To whom arms open wide.

The memories you've made,
With those here and gone.
The smell of a perfume,
The sound of a song.

These cherished things,
Are what give us a home.
It's not in one place,
The heart can roam.

Kids

The mess
The washing
The squabbles
The laundry
The dinners
The packed lunches
The dramas
The school runs
Oh but....
The hugs
The kisses
The laughs
The Dances
The closeness
The jokes
The games
The happiness

Spent

Do you ever feel lost?
Even though you are not away? Like you don't know who to be,
And you don't know what to say.

Your voice is weak and timid,
You carry on to keep the peace.
You smile and nod your head,
Wondering, will it ever cease?

For others drown you out,
and take the best from you.
You give and try so hard,
There's nothing more you can do.

For as soon as you say no,
Or prioritise yourself,
You are labeled as awkward,
Even when it affects your health.

These people pull you down,
And offer nothing in return.
They're only happy when they get their way,
When will you ever learn?

But, for now at this moment,
At least I can see.
I can recognise this behaviour,
And for once, look after me.

Gratitude

I am grateful for my family
My home and my health
I am grateful for my children
My job and my wealth

But just being grateful
It isn't enough you see!
I need to try and spread it around
So it isn't just for me!

Reflections

To reflect is good
And helps us to learn,
But you can't look back
With eyes that yearn.

What happened then
It is done and dusted,
The bad memories
Old and rusted.

Positive things can be
Learned from the past,
So we can move forward
To make memories to last.

Prayers

A prayer is a conversation,
With God or your 'Great One'.
You can thank them for all you have,
And the answers that have come.

You don't have to be a catholic,
Just believe in a greater being.
And know you can talk to them,
They are all-knowing and all-seeing.

Whenever you are lonely or,
Your worries are too much.
You can talk in confidence and hope,
Asking for their healing touch.

There is never any judgement,
Or ridicule to be seen.
God or your Greater Being,
Is always on your team!

Just a Look

Just a look is all it takes
To let someone know you care.
A kindly glance towards them
Lets them know that you are there.

That person could be struggling
Voiceless and alone.
Evening after evening
Unable to pick up the phone.

They could be suffering in silence
Without a shoulder on which to cry.
Sure that the world has forgotten them
Not really understanding why.

So the next time you see that sadness
In someone as you go.
Remember, all it takes is a look
To let them see you care, and you know.

Talk

A problem shared is a problem halved
Isn't that what they say?
Talking over your problems and worries
Can make for a better day.

So, if you find that someone
Who is kind and listens well.
Hold onto that treasure tightly
And listen to them as well.

SELF CARE

Self Healing
Engaging in Me-time
Learning to love yourself
Feelings acknowledged

Caring for yourself
Allowing yourself time
Responding when you are ready
Every Day

The Water

The water is healing
In many ways,
We can watch the river flowing
As it finds a way.

It can cleanse and heal
In the form of a shower,
It can hold you up as you float
And you can feel its power.

It is the essence of our bodies
And keeps us alive,
There is no substitute for water
We need it to survive.

Mummy

There is no one quite like Mummy
You'll learn that as you grow,
She's your steadfast and your rock
When there's trouble, to her you will go.

For Mummy puts you first
You're her first and last thought of the day,
She thinks about you always
For your health and safety she prays.

I know there will be times
When you will wish she wouldn't 'start',
But you will come to learn eventually
She has your best interests at heart.

So when she's growing older
And your patience is about to crack,
Just remember all the times
When Mummy had your back.

For you will never have a Cheerleader
Quite like your Mum,
It is the natural way of things
You are always Number One.

Assumptions

I worry that people don’t like me
I worry about that a lot
I always try to people-please
Whether it upsets me or not

I constantly assume what others think
I never know if it is true
I look at everything negatively
And I can’t blame that on you

I need to change my way of thinking
My patterns need to evolve
Because the way I deal with things now
Well, it's never going to resolve

Because I don’t know what you think
And over that I have no control
But I will make this turnaround
For my mind, body and soul

Progress

One foot in front of the other,
That's the most important thing.
One day at a time,
We'll see what tomorrow brings.

What's done is now done,
There's no point in looking back.
You are moving forward now,
Following new tracks.

So, enjoy today for what it is,
And how important the little things seem.
You will learn to slow down and realise,
How much – just being content - means!

Stay in Your Own Lane

Stay in Your Own Lane
A very wise woman once said
Don't mind what others are doing
There is no space for this in your head

So, you do you
And I'll do me
Then everyone will be happy
To be the person they want to be

Christmas Eve

The anticipation of Santa coming,
The children are so excited.
They're watching the skies with wondrous eyes,
To see if the sleigh can be sighted.

Mummy's in the kitchen,
Warming aromas from within.
She's cooking and singing Christmas Songs,
I love the mood she is in.

Daddy's delivering presents,
To the neighbours and our friends.
Meeting everyone and sharing laughs,
Before this year ends.

But when the evening comes around It is the
best time ever, Because it's just us and close
family,
And we really are together.

Be Like Children

Children have no filter,
They see things in black and white.
'It is what it is!'
There is no need to fight.

They take people as they are,
No judgement or disdain.
They are accepting of all people,
Be they different or plain.

If only we were all like children,
The world would be a better home.
With their capacity for love and acceptance,
We could all learn from them and grow.

www.ingramcontent.com/pod-product-compliance
Lightning Source LLC
Chambersburg PA
CBHW051721130826
49812CB00034B/1288
9789357214827